YOU'VE BEEN WORKING TOO HARD
SO I BROUGHT YOU THIS BOOK

YOU'VE BEEN WORKING TOO HARD
SO I BROUGHT YOU THIS BOOK

OUT TO LUNCH

Compiled by Keith Fallon

STANYAN BOOKS   RANDOM HOUSE

THERE ARE ONLY TWO MEANS OF
FORGETFULNESS KNOWN TO MAN --
WORK AND DRINK -- AND OF THE
TWO, WORK IS THE MORE
ECONOMICAL.

> — ROBERT LYND

I DO NOT LIKE WORK EVEN WHEN
ANOTHER PERSON DOES IT.

- MARK TWAIN

IN LOS ANGELES A MAN NAMED
FAY TURNER SUPPORTS HIS WIFE
AND FOUR DAUGHTERS ON $200
A WEEK. FOR THIS HE LIFTS
465 LB. PHONE BOOTHS AND
INSTALLS THEM. TURNER HAS ONE
LEG; HE USES A CRUTCH FOR
BALANCE. SAYS TURNER, "I'VE
NEVER BEEN UNHAPPY WITH ANY
JOB AS LONG AS I DIDN'T HAVE
TO SIT STILL. AND I DON'T
WANT ANY WELFARE AS LONG AS
I CAN CRAWL."

****

HIRE YOURSELF OUT TO WORK
WHICH IS BENEATH YOU, RATHER
THAN BECOME DEPENDENT ON OTHERS.

- TALMUD

WORK IS THE ONE CONSTANT
IN MY LIFE.

> — LIZA MINNELLI

****

THE CROWNING FORTUNE OF A
MAN IS TO BE BORN TO SOME
PURSUIT WHICH FINDS HIM
EMPLOYMENT AND HAPPINESS,
WHETHER IT BE TO MAKE
BASKETS, OR BROADSWORDS,OR
CANALS, OR STATUES, OR SONGS.

> — RALPH W. EMERSON

****

HARD WORK NEVER KILLED ANYBODY.
BUT THEN AGAIN, RESTING IS
RESPONSIBLE FOR VERY FEW
CASUALTIES.

> — GEORGE GOBEL

I THINK THERE IS FAR TOO MUCH
WORK DONE IN THE WORLD, THAT
IMMENSE HARM IS CAUSED BY THE
BELIEF THAT WORK IS VIRTUOUS.

— BERTRAND RUSSELL

ON BEING A PRINCE:

I LOOK AT IT AS A JOB, AND I
IMAGINE I DO IT AT MUCH THE
SAME PRESSURE I WOULD ANY
OTHER JOB.

— PRINCE PHILIP

****

THE PICTURE THEY (MOST PEOPLE
IN AMERICA) HAVE OF A QUEEN
IS THAT SHE IS LIVING IN A BIG
PALACE AND WEARING A CROWN AND
NOTHING MORE. BUT IT'S A REAL
JOB. IT'S HARD WORK. I WORK
SEVEN HOURS A DAY EVERY DAY.
I'M THE PRESIDENT OF 24
DIFFERENT ORGANIZATIONS...IN
FACT, I'M GETTING GREY HAIRS
ALREADY.

— QUEEN FARAH OF IRAN

I'VE DEVELOPED A SENSE OF
RESPONSIBILITY. I WAS HOPELESSLY
IRRESPONSIBLE BEFORE AND VERY
IDEALISTIC... YOU'VE JUST GOT
TO BE RESPONSIBLE IN MY POSITION.

- HOPE COOKE
  QUEEN OF SIKKIM

****

I'VE BEEN A KING, AND EDITOR,
COMPOSER, FILM DIRECTOR, SAXO-
PHONIST, CHIEF OF STATE -- EVEN
A PRETTY GOOD AMATEUR COOK. I'VE
BEEN PROCLAIMED A NATIONAL HERO
AND DENOUNCED AS A NATION TRAITOR.
WHAT'S LEFT FOR ME ? PERHAPS IT'S
TIME I RETIRED.

- SIHANOUK OF CAMBODIA

WORK! GOD WILLS IT. THAT, IT
SEEMS TO ME, IS CLEAR.

                    — GUSTAVE FLAUBERT

****

GIVE US THE MAN WHO SINGS AT HIS
WORK; WHATEVER HIS OCCUPATION HE
IS EQUAL TO THOSE WHO FOLLOW THE
SAME PURSUIT IN SILENT SULLENNESS.
HE WILL DO MORE IN THE SAME TIME--
HE WILL DO IT BETTER -- HE WILL
PERSEVERE LONGER. ONE IS SCARCELY
SENSIBLE OF FATIGUE WHEN HE
MARCHES TO MUSIC.

                    — THOMAS CARLYLE

****

THE BEST WAY TO GET RID OF YOUR
DUTIES IS TO DISCHARGE THEM.

                    — JOHN RUSKIN

WORK IS LOVE MADE VISIBLE.

- KAHLIL GIBRAN

****

I HAVEN'T REACHED THE POINT
WHERE I SING JUST FOR MONEY,
LIKE A MACHINE. MY EYES GIVE
ME AWAY; I COULDN'T STAND IT
IF I DIDN'T SING WITH MY HEART
AND LOOK PEOPLE IN THE EYES.

- VIKKI CARR

****

LABOR OF THE BODY FREES US
FROM PAINS OF THE MIND -- AND
THUS MAKES THE POOR HAPPY.

- LA ROCHEFOUCAULD

GETTING UP SOME MORNINGS IS JUST
LIKE PUNISHMENT. I'M GOING TO
DIE BEFORE A LOT OF PEOPLE
BECAUSE OF ALL THE SLEEP I'VE
LOST.

> — BARBARA WALTERS

****

WE SPEND OUR MIDDAY SWEAT, OUR
    MIDNIGHT OIL;
WE TIRE THE NIGHT IN THOUGHT,
    THE DAY IN TOIL.

> — FRANCIS QUARLES

****

I PLAN TO CUT DOWN MY WORK LOAD
AND ONLY GO AT IT 15 HOURS A DAY.

> — ROD MCKUEN

ON BURNING THE CANDLE AT BOTH ENDS:

WHO WANTS TO RELAX?
JUST BRING ME MORE WAX!
— LAVONNE MATHISON

WORK THINKS, LAZINESS MUSES.

— JULES RENARD

WITH SOME MEN, WORK IS AS
BESETTING A SIN AS IDLENESS.

- SAMUEL BUTLER

****

AS SOON AS THE RUSH IS OVER
I'M GOING TO HAVE A NERVOUS
BREAKDOWN. I WORKED FOR IT, I
OWE IT TO MYSELF, AND NOBODY'S
GOING TO DEPRIVE ME OF IT.

- CARD ON THE DESK OF
  PEARL BAILEY

****

POSSIBLY WE MIGHT EVEN IMPROVE
THE WORLD A LITTLE, IF WE GOT
UP EARLY IN THE MORNING AND
TOOK OFF OUR COATS TO THE WORK.

- CHARLES DICKENS

WE HAVE TOO MANY PEOPLE WHO LIVE
WITHOUT WORKING, AND ALTOGETHER
TOO MANY WHO WORK WITHOUT LIVING.

- CHARLES R. BROWN

****

THAT'S ONE OF THE TROUBLES TODAY--
PEOPLE ARE AFRAID TO FACE UP TO
RESPONSIBILITIES. WORK IS THE
ONLY THING THAT EVER MADE ANY-
BODY HAPPY. THE NOTION THAT WORK
IS A BURDEN IS A TERRIBLE MISTAKE.

- KATHARINE HEPBURN

TOIL IS THE SIRE OF FAME.

- EURIPIDES

A HARD JOB IS ONE WHICH LEAVES
A FELLOW AS TIRED BEFORE THE
WEEKEND AS AFTER.

- H.F.HENRICHS

****

THE HUMAN FETUS, WE ARE TOLD,
RELIVES THE ENTIRE EVOLUTIONARY
HISTORY OF LIFE, FROM SLIME TO
FISH TO MAMMAL TO FINISHED
HUMAN, IN NINE MONTHS. MUCH THE
SAME THING HAPPENS TO ALL OF
MANKIND EVERY MONDAY MORNING,
BUT WORSE, SINCE THOSE WHO
WORK MUST GO FROM SLIME TO
CIVILIZATION IN A SINGLE
MORNING.

- ERIC JULBER

****

THE TEST OF A VOCATION IS THE
LOVE OF DRUDGERY IT INVOLVES.

- LOGAN PEARSALL SMITH

GO FORTH WITH BRAVE, TRUE
HEARTS, KNOWING THAT FORTUNE
DWELLS IN YOUR BRAIN AND
MUSCLE -- AND THAT LABOR IS THE
ONLY HUMAN SYMBOL OF OMNIPOTENCE.
                    - JAMES A. GARFIELD

****

I TAKE MY WORK WITH ME... I
SIT IN THE CAR AND WORK. I WORK
IN AIRPLANES. WHEREVER I GO IT'S
THERE. I GET IT DONE.
                    - RICHARD NIXON

****

PEOPLE DO NOT SEE THE HARDSHIP
THAT GOES WITH MY CAREER. THEY
DO NOT SEE THE PAIN, THE WORK,
THE DEDICATION. TO TELL YOU THE
TRUTH, I DO NOT LIKE BEING CALLED
"LA DIVINA." I RESENT IT. I AM
MARIA CALLAS. AND I AM ONLY A
WOMAN.   - MARIA CALLAS

THERE ARE SOME DAYS I SIMPLY DO
NOT UNDERSTAND THE UNIVERSE.

- ERIC JULBER

****

MY BOYHOOD EXPERIENCE GAVE ME
A SENSE OF RESPONSIBILITY. IF I
DIDN'T CUT THE FIREWOOD, WE
DIDN'T HAVE FIREWOOD. IF I DIDN'T
CLEAN THE LAMPS, WE DIDN'T HAVE
CLEAN LAMPS.

- GEN. OMAR BRADLEY

SHALLOW MEN BELIEVE IN LUCK.

- RALPH W. EMERSON

WHY SHOULD LIFE ALL LABOR BE?

- ALFRED, LORD TENNYSON

****

TO HANG AROUND -- THAT'S MY
GOAL IN LIFE. I WANT A QUIET LIFE--
ANYTHING TO KEEP MY MIND OFF
WORK. I JUST HATE WORKING. IT's
NOT THAT I'M LAZY; I JUST HAVE A
NATURAL INCLINATION TOWARD
INACTIVITY.

- STANLEY MYRON HANDLEMAN

****

NO MATTER WHAT I'M WORKING ON,
I LIKE TO DO WHAT I'M NOT DOING.

- WOODY ALLEN

FOOLS ARE FOND OF FLITTIN';
AND WISE MEN OF SITTIN'.

- ROBERT BURNS

****

WHEN WORK IS A PLEASURE, LIFE
IS A JOY. WHEN WORK IS A DUTY,
LIFE IS SLAVERY.

- MAXIM GORKI

****

IT TOOK ME FIVE YEARS TO TELL MY
FATHER I DIDN'T LIKE THE FABRICS
BUSINESS.

- LAWRENCE TURMAN, FILM PRODUCER

****

"DON'T YOU EVER FEEL LIKE WORK?"
A LAZY BOY WAS ASKED, AND HE
ANSWERED, "YES,SIR,BUT I DO
WITHOUT."

- SALVADOR DE MADARIAGA

A GOOD MILLSTONE WILL GRIND ANY
GRAIN; A BAD MILLSTONE WILL
GRIND ITSELF AWAY.

- PROVERB

****

IN THE LEXICON OF YOUTH, WHICH
  FATE RESERVES FOR A
BRIGHT MANHOOD, THERE IS NO
  SUCH WORD AS -- FAIL.

- EDWARD BULWER-LYTTON

****

AN OUNCE OF WORK IS WORTH
MANY POUNDS OF WORDS.

- ST.FRANCIS DE SALES

HE THAT DOES NOT GRASP THE THORN
SHOULD NEVER CRAVE THE ROSE.

— ANN BRONTË

WORK KEEPS A MAN ALIVE. I BEEN
WORKING SINCE I WAS TEN YEARS
OLD. THAT'S WHAT'S WRONG WITH
THIS COUNTRY; TOO MANY PEOPLE
DON'T CARE ABOUT WORK ANY MORE
...A MAN'LL RUST OUT FASTER
THAN HE'LL WEAR OUT.

- HARLAND SANDERS (THE "COLONEL")

****

I'VE SEEN IT COME TRUE IN MY OWN
LIFETIME. IF PEOPLE WORK, THEY
CAN HAVE WHAT THEY WANT. PEOPLE
DREAM WHAT THEY CAN ACHIEVE.
IT IS POSSIBLE.

- PAT NIXON

I WAS A CHILD OF POOR PEOPLE,
BUT OUR IDEAL WAS OUR WORK...
THERE'S LOVE, AND WORK, AND
YOUR WIFE. WORK ISN'T TO MAKE
MONEY; YOU WORK TO JUSTIFY LIFE.
THOSE ARE SMALL ACTIONS AND
SIMPLE TRUTHS.

                        — MARC CHAGALL

****

I TOOK TO WRITING AT AN EARLY AGE
TO ESCAPE FROM MEANINGLESS, USE-
LESSNESS, UNIMPORTANCE, INSIGNIFI-
CANCE, POVERTY, ENSLAVEMENT, ILL
HEALTH, DISPAIR, MADNESS AND ALL
MANNER OF OTHER UNATTRACTIVE,
NATURAL AND INEVITABLE THINGS.

                    — WILLIAM SAROYAN

THE BRAIN IS A WONDERFUL ORGAN;
IT STARTS WORKING THE MOMENT YOU
GET UP IN THE MORNING, AND DOESN'T
STOP UNTIL YOU GET INTO THE OFFICE.

– ERIC JULBER

HONEST LABOR BEARS A LOVELY FACE.

- THOMAS DEKKER

****

REX HARRISON AND I LIVED A VERY
ARISTOCRATIC LIFE IN PARIS AND
ON YACHTS AND IN OUR VILLA...
BUT I COULDN'T LIVE ON A YACHT
FOR ONE MORE DAY. I'M WELSH, AND
I COME FROM 500 YEARS OF POVERTY,
WHERE WE HAD TO WORK ALL OUR LIVES,
AND WITHOUT WORK, WITHOUT CREATING
ANYTHING WITH MY OWN LIFE, I JUST
TURNED INTO A VEGETABLE. SO I
GAVE IT UP; BUT IN ITS PLACE, I
FOUND MYSELF.

- RACHEL ROBERTS

A MINISTER NEVER RETIRES .--
ALTHOUGH ADMITTEDLY I CAN'T KEEP
UP THIS CRUSADE WORK ALL MY LIFE.
BUT I HOPE TO BE PREACHING AND
WRITING ON THE DAY I DIE.

- BILLY GRAHAM

****

AS A REMEDY AGAINST ALL ILLS --
POVERTY, SICKNESS, AND MELANCHOLY--
ONLY ONE THING IS ABSOLUTELY
NECESSARY: A LIKING FOR WORK.

- CHARLES BAUDELAIRE

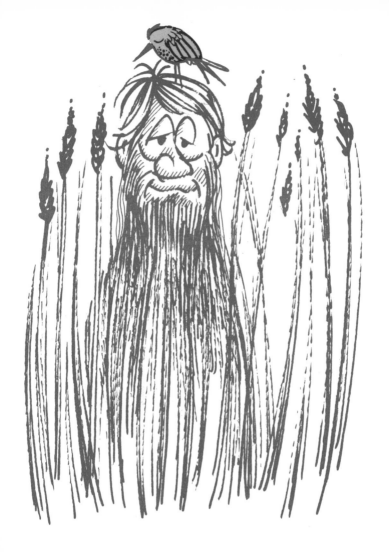

SOME PEOPLE WHO GET CREDIT FOR
BEING PATIENT ARE JUST TOO
LAZY TO START ANYTHING.

— JOHN CASS

AFTER A TEN-DAY VACATION
WITH HER HUSBAND:

WHEN I SAW HIM OUT IN THE WOODS
HITTING PINE CONES WITH A BROOM-
STICK, I REALIZED IT WAS TIME TO
GET BACK TO THE TOUR.

- MRS.LEE TREVINO

****

I WOULDN'T WORK SO HARD IF SOMEONE
WOULD PLAY WITH ME.

- ROD MCKUEN

FAME, MY DEAR CHILDREN, IS NOT
AN EASY MANTLE TO WEAR.

- PEARL BAILEY

CHRISTMAS CARD FOR EMPLOYEES

YOU BETTER WATCH OUT,
YOU BETTER NOT CRY,
YOU BETTER NOT POUT,
I'M TELLING YOU WHY,

IT WON'T LOOK GOOD ON YOUR
PERSONNEL RECORD,

AS MY CAREER HAS ADVANCED, I HAVE
FOUND IT A GREAT ANTIDOTE TO
SELF-ADULATION TO VISIT THE SANTA
MONICA NEIGHBORHOOD WHERE I
WASHED THE WINDOWS OF A DRUG STORE
AND SWEPT OUT THE STOCK ROOM OF A
DRY-GOODS STORE.

— GLENN FORD

"A FAIR DAY'S WAGES FOR A FAIR DAY'S WORK"; IT IS AS JUST A DEMAND AS GOVERNED MEN EVER MADE OF GOVERNING. IT IS THE EVERLASTING RIGHT OF MAN.

– THOMAS CARLYLE

****

THE BARTENDERS' UNION HAS TOLD THE BOSSES THAT A BARTENDER'S BIRTHDAY IS SOMETHING SACRED AND HE SHOULD BE PAID $45 THAT DAY RATHER THAN $22.

– EARL WILSON

WORK SPARES US FROM THREE
GREAT EVILS; BOREDOM, VICE
AND NEED.

> — VOLTAIRE

****

WORK IS WHAT YOU DO SO THAT
SOME TIME YOU WON'T HAVE TO
DO IT ANY MORE.

> — ALFRED POLGAR

****

BUSINESS? IT'S QUITE SIMPLE.
IT'S OTHER PEOPLE'S MONEY.

> — ALEXANDRE DUMAS, THE YOUNGER

INDUSTRY IS THE ROOT OF ALL UGLINESS.

                    - OSCAR WILDE

****

ANYONE CAN DO ANY AMOUNT OF WORK,
PROVIDED IT ISN'T THE WORK HE IS
SUPPOSED TO BE DOING AT THE MOMENT.

                  - ROBERT BENCHLEY

****

I COULD GO FOREVER NOT WORKING.
I DON'T ENJOY WORK. I WOULDN'T
WORK AT ALL IF I DIDN'T HAVE AN
ELEGANT BALLROOM AND WIFE TO
SUPPORT.

                  - ROBERT MITCHUM

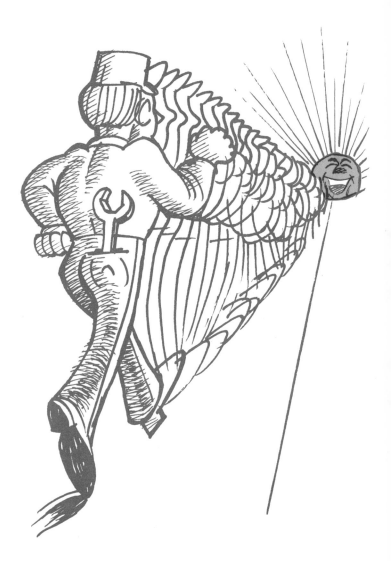

ONE MUST WORK, NOTHING BUT WORK.
AND ONE MUST HAVE PATIENCE.

- AUGUSTE RODIN

THE GENIUS OF SUCCESS IS STILL
THE GENIUS OF LABOR. IF HARD WORK
IS NOT ANOTHER NAME FOR TALENT,IT
IS THE BEST POSSIBLE SUBSTITUTE
FOR IT.

> — JAMES A.GARFIELD

****

THE ACHIEVER IS THE ONLY INDIVIDUAL
WHO IS TRULY ALIVE... I SEE NO
DIFFERENCE BETWEEN A CHAIR AND THE
MAN WHO SITS IN THE CHAIR UNLESS
HE IS ACCOMPLISHING SOMETHING.

> — GEORGE ALLEN
> FORMER L.A.RAMS COACH

DISCIPLINE MEANS ETHICS, IT MEANS
STYLE, IT MEANS MANNERS. IT MEANS
BEING ON TIME TO WORK. IT MEANS
EFFICIENCY. IT MEANS GIVING A
DAMN FOR THE JOB YOU DO. HALF THE
PEOPLE TODAY WOULD DIE IF THEY
HAD TO TOE THE LINE.

- ARTHUR TREACHER

****

I COULD HAVE RETIRED SIX YEARS AGO
AT FULL PAY. BUT I DECIDED THAT
THE LORD HAD BEEN GOOD TO ME, AND
I WANTED TO GIVE THE PUBLIC THE
BENEFIT OF MY EXPERIENCE.

- JULIUS J.HOFFMAN
FEDERAL DISTRICT JUDGE

'TIS THE PART OF A WISE MAN TO
KEEP HIMSELF TODAY FOR TOMORROW,
AND NOT VENTURE ALL HIS EGGS
IN ONE BASKET.

— MIGUEL DE CERVANTES

LIKE EVERY MAN OF SENSE AND GOOD
FEELING, I ABOMINATE WORK.

- ALDOUS HUXLEY

****

HAPPINESS IS NEARLY ALWAYS A
REBOUND FROM HARD WORK.

- DAVID GRAYSON

****

WROTE ANSWERS TO ONE OR TWO
LETTERS WHICH HAVE BEEN LYING
ON MY DESK LIKE SNAKES, HISSING
AT ME FOR MY DILATORINESS..

- SIR WALTER SCOTT

IT PROVES, ON CLOSE EXAMINATION,
THAT WORK IS LESS BORING THAN
AMUSING ONESELF.

- CHARLES BAUDELAIRE

A GEOLOGIST SAID THE EARTH MAY
EXPLODE IN A BILLION YEARS OR SO,
AND SOME PEOPLE ARE ALREADY
USING HIS PREDICTION AS AN EXCUSE
NOT TO LOOK FOR A JOB.

                    - BEVINS JAY

****

THE COMMON MAN THINKS OF COMFORT.

                    - CONFUCIUS

****

GET ON YOUR BUTT.

                    - FRED ALLEN

BY MEANS OF WORK ONE EXCEEDS
ONE'S CAPACITIES.

> — JEAN ROSTAND

****

TO THE RIGHT SORT OF MEN AND
WOMEN, HAPPINESS IS FOUND IN
THE ROUTINE ITSELF, NOT IN
DEPARTURES FROM IT.

> — WILLIAM LYON PHELPS

YOU WORK THAT YOU MAY KEEP
PEACE WITH THE EARTH AND THE
SOUL OF THE EARTH.

- KAHLIL GIBRAN

****

HOW MUCH EASIER OUR WORK WOULD
BE IF WE PUT FORTH AS MUCH EFFORT
TRYING TO IMPROVE THE QUALITY
OF IT AS MOST OF US DO TRYING
TO FIND EXCUSES FOR NOT PROPERLY
ATTENDING TO IT.

- GEORGE BALLINGER

ALWAYS STRICT DISCIPLINE. EVERY
MORNING AT WORK BY EIGHT, STOP AT
12:30. NOTHING INTERFERES. I WALK
THREE MILES. NOTHING INTERFERES.
AFTER THAT, I DO WHATEVER I FEEL
SPUNKY ABOUT...

- RUTH GORDON

I HAVE NEVER SEEN A CAT THAT
COULDN'T CALM ME DOWN JUST BY
WALKING SLOWLY PAST MY CHAIR.

        - ROD MCKUEN

WHAT WE CALL "CREATIVE WORK"
OUGHT NOT TO BE CALLED WORK AT
ALL, BECAUSE IT ISN'T... I
IMAGINE THAT THOMAS EDISON
NEVER DID A DAY'S WORK IN HIS
LAST FIFTY YEARS.

– STEPHEN LEACOCK

THIS IS AN INSECURE BUSINESS.
YOU'RE ONLY AS GOOD AS YOUR LAST
SHOW. IT'S NOT LIKE GOING TO THE
OFFICE EVERY DAY AND KNOWING THAT
AFTER 20 YEARS THEY'LL GIVE YOU
THE GODDAM WATCH.

— JOHNNY CARSON

I TRAIN BY TAKING IT EASY.

> \- LEE TREVINO

****

I WANT TO KEEP FIT, YOUNG, INTERESTED AND HAPPY. I'VE BEEN SHOVED AROUND ALL MY LIFE, AND NOW I WANT TO DO THINGS WITHOUT ANYBODY CROWDING ME AND THE PHONE RINGING.

> \- LYNDON JOHNSON

WORK IS A FORM OF NERVOUSNESS.

- DON HEROLD

****

I BELIEVE THERE IS THE TRAGEDY OF
A MAN WHO WORKS VERY HARD AND
NEVER GETS WHAT HE WANTS. AND THEN
I BELIEVE THERE IS THE EVEN MORE
BITTER TRAGEDY OF A MAN WHO
FINALLY GETS WHAT HE WANTS AND
FINDS OUT HE DOESN'T WANT IT.

- HENRY KISSINGER

REST IS THE SWEET SAUCE OF LABOR.

- PLUTARCH

****

THE JOY OF LIVING COMES FROM
ACTION, FROM MAKING THE ATTEMPT,
FROM THE EFFORT, NOT THE SUCCESS.

- SIR FRANCIS CHICHESTER

IT ISN'T THE THING YOU DO, DEAR,
    IT'S THE THING YOU LEAVE UNDONE
THAT GIVES YOU A BIT OF A HEARTACHE
    AT SETTING OF THE SUN.

                    — MARGARET SANGSTER